G-D, SLEEP, AND CHAOS

Alan Fyfe

G-D, SLEEP, AND CHAOS

PART ONE: ELEGIES FOR A TUESDAY AFTERNOON

Eulogy for Hasan

My grief wakes up and phones a small town in Turkey. My grief accepts bribes in fresh fruit. My grief beats its imaginary friend. My grief calls out for food from the concrete factory. My grief owns a Citroën but won't tell anyone. My grief sends angry letters to dead politicians. My grief scratches the four-letter word tattooed on its knuckles.

My grief is an ibis scrabbling through trash looking for comparison. My grief is under the credit card in the wallet of a flea beneath its wing. My grief is the bird's call which remembers Egypt.

My grief can't hear me or the waterfall we're standing next to. It can't see the cascade soaking the worn volcanic rock. But it can climb down the uneven face, careful in its cheap shoes, drink the clean water that runs over the lowest stones in its cupped hand, plunge in up to the wrist, and flex its digits feeling for angel's teeth in the sand at the bottom.

A Hill Outside Yanchep

A swell in the geography
is a lower jaw
five months after
a punch in the face.

Blackened tooth stumps;
scatter, evidence,
on the vanished border
once named 'tree line.'

Pig-tail smoke curls
exhale between grains;
black dirt burnt white;
breath of yesterday's visitor.

The quiet is roaring, wheezing,
dreaming of methane.
Ruthless silence,
in the days after birdsong.

A Funeral in Pinjarra

Haul my half dead carcass to a teleconference,
so I can tell everyone I'm not afraid,
even though I've always been afraid.

Afterwards, lay the sequined shroud
and roll me through Pinjarra strapped
to a fibreglass cow with casters in its hooves.

Bake cakes for the children,
throw fruit and nut
on the heads of my friends.

Prepare the pink meat,
cubes of cheddar,
and varicoloured cocktail onions.

Arrange them, skewered on toothpicks
in sacred geometry on the scratched PCV platter
and eat them in remembrance of me.

Let the pipe band play Fuck the Police
and all voices join;
ringing, rapturous, pointless.

Scurrilous rumours of me must abound—
let them grow Icarus wings
and appear as sparks over a dreaming shopping centre.

Spill all the tea!
Fine leaf & tip liquor flowing in
steaming gushes of my every flirt with evil.

Give uncles 5-meter clearances for anecdotes
and store toilet paper for whatever tears might fall;
for my grave goods, 15 rolls, I'll miss you too.

Place little dolls in rows to enact
plots from childhood space-operas
when rouges knew the innards of machines—

when we too knew how to plumb the workings
and deduce, in polyphony, how every engine
could crest the galaxy if only kindness could win.

And you must face the crowd of thousands I fully assume will gather,
and you must lie extravagantly about how unafraid I was—
the kind of lies that made me smile,
the kind I always leaned in close to hear you say.

Gilgul

When I was a ghost, I was cold. I died in the red cotton pants
I slept in—no shirt (schlepping fat-bellied and exposed all
over some half and half afterlife).

The canapes at the wake, glossy and spoiling in the sun,

No hunger, no heartbreak. But who could have known I'd
need to bring a good coat (He died as he lived, they said,
unprepared and badly dressed)?

a scent that pleases the L-rd, who takes them as titbits for
Leviathan's bowl.

The feeling was mild—say, that minor chill you feel around
three in the morning (when you can't get back to sleep
because the sky is too beautiful).

Oh, Most-High of hemp-ropes and signals and overly expensive
dental repairs;

But, three hundred years on, small irritation becomes hell
(the paperwork came in triplicate from the Book of Life—he
doesn't *exactly* deserve hell).

creator of men with velvet pictures and abandoned latex gloves by
the roadside;

They were sending me back to flesh (the college of spirits
confer on my past—whiner; eater; masturbator; it's a sin to
stub out a cigarette on a white-gum).

preserve them from frost, Hashem, they have too much skin.

At the river, the angel of forgetting signed off (now let
the water enter your nostrils, your lungs, emerge clean of
recollection on the far bank).

I see you in the exhausts of cars and the thin mist over glass pipes;

The ice prickle flared as I waded in (liquid on crackling
plasma). I ignored the angel—held my breath (don't tell G-d,
but I remember everything).

I am grateful for every past—let my brothers drink at the graveside.

Because I Found a 45 Minute Window to Stop for Death

after 'Because I could not stop for Death' *by Emily Dickinson*

May you come down the street borrowing and borrowing and borrowing hats from the neighbours, so that they cover you—bucket-hat; flat-cap; fedora; babushka-scarf—until the hats form the rainbow coat you will take me under.

May you come a little past two on a Sunday while I'm weeding, when the light is that ochre kissed shade of perfect for the frame shot of Marlon Brando carking it in the Godfather.

May you come off the front end of a red truck chewing up the Mandurah Bypass with loads of bricks and tatters of wind-torn plastic wrap humming in the speed-force—one of those old ovoid fenders—the driver on his third day sleepless.

May you come as a beautiful stranger singing Sally MacLennane round my door deep after a sensible bedtime, with all the dental-veneers paid for and set on your shark-bite charm.

May you come flying and farting out of a tavern carpark in Rockingham, so drunk you've seen the reflection of your soul in the surface of an ammonia clouded aluminium toilet cistern—may you beat me unconscious with a tender hand.

May you always be coming, truest follower, so I remember to take my honey in a heaving teaspoon in every sunny kitchen from the span of yesterday to not-yet.

Ned Kelly

The most interesting thing about Ned Kelly is that I thought of the name of his horse while I peered over the fence at late twilight when the trees in my neighbours' yard had become silhouettes and all I could pick out was the heart shape Kambarang buds that will grow to their limits then dry and carpet our driveway in only eight months and the name of his horse was music.

PART TWO: THE VOID STARES BACK

Want

And who was it, before plans for the flood were finalized, that prayed for it?

Message

The digital photo is a trick of light
halfway through a life of Augusts
when violet Chinese apples dropped
from lax branches overhead
and clunked on the glass table.

ON MISUNDERSTANDINGS

After the L-rd took out the tower
the erstwhile masons all gathered
for the welfare queue in Morley.

Muted greens and back-of-the-eyes
fluorescent headaches, rows of
armchairs, slogans on vinyl signs.

Rabbits

Rabbits don't have a fastidious language
to recount, to their children, the taste
of a very fine cabbage, or the excitement
of its theft from a guarded vegetable patch.

Only, puddled for warmth in a hutch,
sniffing for petrichor, their skin knows
that tingling at the follicles is the storm
as their parents' skin knew, just the same.

THE BIN TRUCK SAID

Bow-bellied-behemoth snail barging,
heavy on the asphalt of Charles Street,
a mid-July at 2 P.M that apes twilight;
grey cumulus luck-dragons eat the sun.
Axles strain and talk; hydraulic arms
whinge and gossip; click clack bin-lids
do staccato paragraphs on lost rat-food.
                              The machine declaims in
Wookie whines and pig-squeal dialect
half-words, like dreaming on varenicline.
And, whatever petty deity I've pissed off now
has made the bin truck whisper all my secrets to the street.

The bin truck speaks of loneliness in
an overcrowded house; the bin truck
quick-flashes crumpled medical results;
the bin truck knows everything I eat.
My intimacies it takes into its private self
and fifteen hundred other intimacies too.
Co-mingled, recycled, composted communal
cradle of the neighbourhood's yesterdays.
                              Great diesel fired leveller
digests all equally in its creaky iron gut,
wagyu scraps and nugget fat just the same.
Lifts a fleeting week from the driveway's mouth
then turns and disappears where the corner meets the rail-track.

PATIENCE

I'm
just
here
chewing
the
weatherboard
off
the
side
of
the
house

Two Visitation Dreams

1.

The long-bodied angel,
wrapped in a charcoal trench coat,
soles under patent leather
floating fifteen centimetres proud
of the gleaming rail-track,
                                        raised a hand,
                                        pointed south
                                        with the flow
                                        of a clear, trickling river.
I followed along the bank
of damp salt and pepper dirt,
heading into a past
playing out on a bare mudflat—
top layer crusted and jigsaw cracked
                                        under antique sun
                                        (I have seen,
                                        I am witness).
Shadow of a child's brown hand elongates
on whitened soil like a movie screen.
A voice from behind the upturned palm
speaks the first human word ever uttered;
and the word means warmth, proximity, wet.
                                        And the first word
                                        is 'milk'.

2.

The long-bodied angel,
wrapped in a pearl-grey chiton,
hamburger-raw bare feet
disconnected by eight inches
from the dust haze earth,
raised a hand,
pointed north
along the flow
of a turgid, stinking aqueduct.
I followed the pockmarked PVC
that sided and retained the water,
heading into a future
playing out on the edge of a city,
with a jagged, pain-wrought skyline,
like bones after blunt trauma
(I have seen,
I am witness).
Ember glow on the far horizon—
looming, approaching, increasing.
A crowd of refugees shoulder close,
choral humming the last human word uttered;
and the last word means cold, proximity, dry.
And the last word
is 'hold'.

PART THREE: G-D, SLEEP, AND CHAOS

First Problema

Where were we going with this again?

Ocean

Remember when you wrote that poem? On the first line you levered two ideas in five words. On the second line you decided it was a holiday. By the third line you sold your ego to the universe. But the fourth line had you phoning for travel insurance. You broke on the stanza and made a love letter by gluing cardboard shapes together.

You were open as a country gate to start again. The fifth line went for seventeen pages. You decided this was free verse. The sixth line took a year and you celebrated with a cake. The next two lines came out together. Paired and twisted. You worked so hard to make them not rhyme. The rhymes defied all phonics and stuck to the blank spots. You broke on the stanza and had three children and four jobs.

Did it need four-line stanzas in the first place? The ninth line was your finest work. There was no answer in the tenth. The eleventh line was a naked lie. The twelfth was an infection. The thirteenth saw the welt spread. At fourteen lines it split open. Cloudy liquor-puris blotted the page. You broke on the stanza and sent a stern email to the council.

You were only fourteen and so damn lonely. You wrote to the shadow behind the picture frame. You gave up on the seventeenth line. The manuscript had grown too fat to lift. All authority borrowed from immortality had expired. You broke before the stanza and cooked a familiar meal. You sat with your favourite drug, sleepy on the patio at six, watching the long night roll in off the ocean.

Euthyphro Dilemma

G-d comes up to me at Perth Central. Bums a smoke. Looks about fifty-six. Though time hasn't been kind. He'd been waiting for a bus. Lost track looking at his phone. Infinite grace lost down a you tube hole. This is G-d you remember. He knows the next bus is running late.

His feet are bare and dirty. I offer him thongs. New double pluggers I got at Target. I don't know how you worship. I like to have thongs ready. He waves them off. Kind of you, but the ground's what wants protection from me, not the other way round. Is there anything I can do for you? Just keep me company until the bus comes. Some hash if you've got it. The omniscient mind gets busy.

There's an issue I'm having. You're omnipotent but the bus is still late. The most-high nods his everywhere head. Silvery dandruff floats to the pavement like manna. His phone rings. The seraphim are calling. Their pay's infinity late. He never answers.

I can see where you're having trouble. Try doing this job for ten minutes. I could make the bus run on time. But do you take me for some fascist? Imagine knowing you can tune the clockwork to a micron. Then also knowing that the bus driver has her reasons.

St John's Wort

A pinching wind will sting your face; while waiting for the pot to boil; until it's dry and starts to burn; and when it burns you'll wonder why; you set the pot to boil at all; you won't remember what good food; you dreamed up when you started out; it must have been a butter crumb; it must have been a homely smell; it must have meant a time to sit; and edit half your yesterdays.

The wind's still going hard and high; the pot's still reeking from the burn; you're hearing distant Wu Tang Clan; remember losing time on that; you left the lost-times in the grass; ten years ago or maybe more; and now it's more a brittle thing; a stem dried wholly to the core.

You'll say it's just like St John's Wort; a class A weed you kill at work; it clogs up every nature strip; and bears up proudly in the drought; still you asked around to find; the stuff's put to some decent use; the herb's been tested double blind; and double blind was blind enough; to feed the black-dog off to sleep; and thin the plump suburban shame; a strong green life that thrives alone; and never asks a gardener's touch; so happiness grows everywhere; and everywhere we fight it off.

A Psalm for Esther

What is a hamantasch? A sacred vulva filled with black seeds. A food, source of nourishment, which we make with our hands reflecting our (women's) felt sense of self-containment, of creativity and generativity.

—Susan Schur, *Womantasch,* Lilith Magazine, March 1998.

Holy baking for Adar when through strident chlorine fumes of oven cleaner bursts the angel of forgetting with a passing resemblance to Amy Winehouse only fifteen meters tall and when the dough is formed in triangle shapes she declaims in the syntax of West Pinjarra which was never still and small that this is the story of cunts and that cunts birthed every one of you but sometimes a biscuit is just a biscuit and centred with a glob of jam like sticky truth so she replies cunts are the victory and the wave crest and the G-d place for such thin traditions of baking were barely born when she saw Canaanite women lay notes at the feet of Inanna then popping open a document box of still buried stele which record the secret breath of history she reveals that G-d was in the footnotes after all.

After Pittsburgh

The names of the slain at L'Simcha were Joyce Fienberg, Richard Gottfried, Rose Mallinger, Jerry Rabinowitz, Cecil & David Rosenthal, Bernice & Sylvan Simon, Daniel Stein, Melvin Wax, and Irving Younger. Their memory for a blessing.

Everyone talks about light. You can bathe in light. You can run towards it. An army of novelists wrote the domestic bible on the uses of light. So plain at its work. Through branches. Through windows. Lit faces. Lit calendars. Revelation's song and dance. Old lines for a gaudy spring.

The missing vowel from G-d can't show up in the light. That O hums more in the spaces between the furniture and the wall. Keeping diplomacy with the roaches. Covering the particular beauty of a moth's corpse. Singing kaddish for the blessed memory of fleas.

Hard profanity, to trap this morning on paper. Even more, lending phonics to the unseen. Many thanks, for the light that comes to those of us left. Many thanks, for the dark which makes the outlines.

Second Problema

Why would I get out of bed?

Box

Your whole family can be traced to half a supermarket aisle in a country your grandmother barely heard of. The shelves are piled with confused jigsaw pieces and no one to even collate the colours and edges. The key picture from the puzzle's container was buried with Gilgamesh and hasn't been sighted since. You don't know why you understand how the fragments fit exactly in their pattern except that you saw the top of the box in a dream.

Trains

One of the most frequent dreams is about trains. There's this time on the Midland line, hurtling between two stations, it takes two kilometres to stop at that speed. I see the nose-cone bloodied up, the way it was that night when I worked at the Mandurah depot, we to put on hazard suits to clean it. But I was awake then. Or there's the Merredin railway museum. I stopped there with Yitzhak. The age when he was still invested in Thomas the Tank-Engine. All the hoary steamers. Sorry, son, the diesels won. I was awake then too. No. The dream is of too many bodies packed up in a bare carriage—so tight we're sweating though it's snowing outside. I have it every few months.

Elephant

Dream of the elephant   the elephant's on a stage   the stage curtains from Katanning town hall   saw my only pantomime   elephant knocks over the props   paper furniture made for school dioramas   breakfast news with elephant   elephant knocks over buildings in village   I've leaked in the future   less generous Austrians contend   lots of people dream about elephants   elephants knock things over   elephants can't help it   this is what dream elephants are for   nudge it all you like Sigmund   the centre holds just fine   we're all prophets

Poplar

for Channa

I wake up in the tropical grove at the university two weeks after the funeral. It has been ten years since I visited and everything has changed. I'm scrabbling through the ferns at the edge of a garden bed, looking for the poplar.

A security guard appears through the sunning leaves of a prehistoric succulent and tells me to put the smoke out. He looks like Richard Gere from that awful 1985 King David TV biopic and I'm not actually smoking.

Pretending I don't hear him, I start to walk into the garden beds which seem to be expanding, stretching so that I can't see the end. He tries to get my attention again, his voice expanding, he says the smoke is getting everywhere.

It was somewhere near here when I left, the image clear as hour ago, a brass plaque fixed to the trunk with Latin species name and a fork jammed in the side, protruding like a coat hook. I tell him I have to see it. I have to see the tree with the brass plaque.

Of course, I can't find it without the plaque. I don't know what a poplar looks like, I only ever read the word in a book. The guard resigns authority and lights his own cigarette, calling after me—What's the matter, champ, misplaced your harp?

Commerce

Odd how rare it is to see people with animal heads these days, particularly because three percent of the customers at the home-centre are dream figures. Or, at least between one thirty and four on a Saturday, when afternoon naps are peaking. Weaving in and out for TVs and hair-straighteners and vegan-fudge; personal representations and complete psychic constructs; manifested and sent to the concrete strip mall by dreamers. At Canning Home-World, you can't tell them from real people until you bump into one and pass right through. They're mostly locals from the new brick-and-tin suburbs, flowering out from the tilt-slab CBD, who passed under on a sunny couch and got no further than where they'd been this morning.

Third Problema

Why are you even like this?

You'll need to track the substance across the globe. Shipping movements, reputable suppliers, police interceptions. A little Friedman will help, the flux of supply and demand will tell you how to set the clocks, and pinpoint locations where horrific chasms of opportunity are opening. After the thrill of the first transactions, you'll need lay out strategies for a long relationship with the product. Selling some will keep your own larder stocked. There is a sense in which it needs to be an inductive artform too. Dishonesty is a natural way to protect interests, and discerning what truth lies tell is vital. But, for the two percent of you that still dreams, the rest must be a pure node of the market. The process is analytic. Take the fit-pack you are using for example—the notated, exacting needle, the little vial of clear, sterile water.

I Talked to a Coffee

I love you, coffee, because you remind me of death. You're the colour my lungs will be when they cut me open. Wrap me up like that young cowboy from the song. Send the police round to see my brothers. The meat might be a slice too cured. Not useful for medical experiments. Maybe cut scenes for anti-smoking ads. Maybe have me stuffed. Dress me as a human Ibis. Bolt me to the roof to scare the neighbours. Don't condescend me, coffee. I know where we're going with this. It's just, I got my face close. It was written after that. Please know I'm grateful. Someone told me to use ground wattle seeds, and that stinks of avoidance. You kill me a little every day, but with such a loving hand.

Guns

Sharp noises on TV. Go ahead, make my day. I turn it off, but I'm not averse. I could take fruit to your sick aunt. I could eat that experimental cake you baked. Someone said you shouldn't put avocado in cake, but you didn't listen, you never listen. It's ok, I'll eat. Maybe a picnic, a walk through the peppermint myrtles, where the shaggy fronds stroke the grass. Leave the toolkit hanging off your hatstand, we won't need it where we're going, up to the river's edge for the secret noises. I swear there's little marsupials unknown to science. We can give them names that no one's guessed. We'll look at their fragile little bodies and learn to love life that way, just like that film you like, the one where the bad-guy looks at a fragile little body and learns to love life. Look, it's all here. I've made a list of things to make you happy. But it wasn't exactly happiness you were talking about, was it?

TO A FRIEND

I want to stab you in the eye because I care about you   I can
see it clean through now   you're in the sunken garden singing
psalms   more alive at one a.m. than in judgey daylight   you
show me the bag with little mountains   where you keep your
tomorrow   and six vague Thursdays   glassy edged slopes
held back from geologic growth   like those little trees   they
bind the limbs with wires   each grown after a model   Ben
Nevis   Glyder Fawr   Bluff's Knoll   Mount Warning   each
drying you out on the climb   you held out for the peaks   and
paid hard cash for license   I worry   alone with a glass of
wine   looking through the dirty front window   I worry about
you   watching night chew up Maylands   I worry the big
world will eat you too   so I want to stab you in the eye with a
compass   watch the intraocular fluid leak out   because you
won't take care of yourself

A Letter to Bukowski from Maylands

what structure of words to say two friends opened up a bookstore on eighth avenue and it feels safe to have books nearby but the new benches make us want to shout at something because they took away the type you can sleep on and replaced them with twin wooden armchairs on a petite angle into each other like the stage set for an interview

you know that type of shouting as exemplified by the family who dragged a mattress up behind the supermarket and the father gets up and roars the victory of waking out over guilford rd in shapeless syllables of pure anger and praise right near the corner we passed last week talking about suicide in the bright morning

nice to be outside after we kept the windows closed past ten until the walls cried to the L-rd for tobacco but i can't attend too long while two friends who opened a bookstore on eighth avenue talk about rents because i think about my rent then worry if you're making rent then go home and write terrible verse about prices

notice us you saintly bastard as we perch on the northern bank with fighting black swans marking out the land of popper's exception just i and my singular thou on the birdshit planks under publicliesinart taped over the theft where everything can be viewed at a safe distance as fragile and useless and jaundice sick to the point of beauty

PART FOUR: FOURTEEN LOVE POEMS

RELATIONSHIPS

It is time to leave
when the sound of chewing is
unbearably loud.

Ether

Call in the Sunday wind.
Lend energy to old women
whose dresses blow up
a thousand panicked Marilyns
at every backyard luncheon.
Raise kites and wreck them.
Carry shopping bags
secret notes
and all of yesterday's autumn.

Discourse mightily
on the smallness of her hands.
Put good words all around her.
Cough from your fifteenth cigarette
before creeping noon. Light another.
And, for G-d's sake,
show some tiny kindness.
Tomorrow weighs a tonne.

Black Box

Two entirely naked people
clothed in the brocade dignity
of each other's pleasure.

Fingertips run along the curve
of gravity, imagining this
could be the ideal touch.

Chancing on sunken gardens in
accidents of flesh, discovering
unknown nations of skin.

The feeling of the touch is a
conceit of the giver. Could this be
it—the first ideal touch?

Two locked box minds in the dim
streetlight filtering through the curtains,
attempting communion.

A Doomed Marriage

Out of the eater something to eat
Out of the strong something sweet

—Judges 14:14

Dream of Samson at the task
bent hard to the maw
pushing out in all directions
Sun sharp on temples
breath of the old blonde beast
wet on his wide neck

Composing riddles for the feast
Jealousy already a buzz
behind straining reddening eyes
Killing before the celebration
trained to kill and used to killing
The animal breaks in his hands

Beowulf at the Terminal

On St George's Terrace waiting for the no. 32 green dragon.

A woman catches a drop of saliva that escapes the mash
of a jam doughnut she's been working with her dentures.
Runs the berry tinted liquid over woolly, cracked lips with
a tight index finger. For ten seconds he loves her more than
warmth.

They hear cat-cry whine of the axle and go rigid together
with a helpless fear of missing out on the promised end.
Raw and hopeful in the contracting seconds before the
dragon comes.

Crystal

note Zarrah

a air said when

leave upper to you

to the me fuck

forget of one off

don't cabinet night forever

important the will by and

is in it be a sign

Rhythm itself addicted to fire it

4files become a on lots

3smoke ever drug the of

2floating I with salt love

1Sorrid if beautiful name a flats Libertine

A Pear with an Excellent Flavour

after Sigmund Freud's Wolf-Man

You bite past the thin
yellow striped skin
firm, grainy flesh
dissolves in your mouth
The juice is heartbreak sweet
the aroma is the bark and the bloom
You are wholly alive
—ignited—expanding
You are very young

Though you can't be aware of it now
nothing will ever taste this good again

She works, kneeling
at the riverbank
shoulders narrow
drawing water
pushing strands
of melancholy brown
back under her grandmother scarf

You recall the weight
of the pear in your hand

Expelled from the garden
before you've even tasted

Smaller

She was a pinpoint
a flare somewhere
near the horizon
shouting grave
urgent transmissions
he was never built
to properly receive.

Airport

Someone parked their bike,
covered in a grey nylon,
on the wasteland tarmac
far west of the long
domestic terminal.

Someone cleaned the windows;
long strokes, veins
contracted on the wrist,
right heel cocked
like a ballerina stepping on pointe,
turning a shoulder to the sky
just to reach
high enough.

Someone laid the light tiles
at the climate neutral
automated check in;
and someone picked the tiles
to shine under the buffer,
to be smooth and cold,
to never catch, offend,
or confront the eye.

Someone checked the instruments
and engaged the machine
to lift over the moving world—
alight across the hungry distance,
rest, refuel, return.

Wall

On Monday morning
took care of some organisational concerns,
so no one would be very surprised if I didn't leave the house.

My schedule thus clear,
I floated over to rest on the red pillows
and invested my attention in the grubby wall behind the woodstove.

Bubbles of paint, chipped
history of food grease, smoke, trapped heat.
I swear, round one in the afternoon, the unpainted part twitched.

She sent her missive
in blue light through the crystal window.
The wall seemed about to seethe, but I turned my attention to her.

Filing System

for Rachel

There's a place, off to the side of your liver,
where you keep that spiky thing;
the one you'd rather not touch.
But it worries and scrapes at the flesh wall,
so much like a fresh, crusted sore,
that you can't help but to prod.

There's a dusty place on top of the wardrobe,
you keep your grandmother's journal;
faint pastel pages, floral background.
Still a scent about it, some antique bouquet,
but you know nothing about perfumes,
so you fill gaps with conceits—musk.

There's a page, far on in the aromatic journal,
where the thin wrist forced the pen
so hard, it ghosted several sheets.
One line, tall as five of her lighter strokes:
I CAN'T FUCKING TAKE IT!
After that, there's only recipes.

River

In the morning, double rainbow
at a distance, past the river.
The sun break made the heat rise
and the aching house frame shivered.

There's her body at his body
and there's power in skin to skin.
Shards and crystals on the water—
light on rivers far within.

Smash

We loved like divine wind pilots
hand blue on the gears, teeth clenched
hard enough to grind a coarse powder which
we will use as emery to sharpen our blades

We loved at 400 kph pointed straight
at a drift block wall that scraped the ceiling
of infinity—dwarfed our fragile vehicle
pushed harder at the pedal

We loved with our heels against
the scorching stone of a bench grinder
striking sparks off into the blank page
darkness of G-d's huge workshop.

for the Moon

I have often sat with her
alone on the brick step
wondering how her tricks
never lose their currency

with a cup of black tea
warmed by star-anise
and her monthly show
a pool ball disappearing
into a pocket made of the void

I know how she feels about me
neither of us bothered to grow up

PART FIVE: VARIOUS SELF DESTRUCTIONS

A Glass on top of a Book

Frost clouds
blue backdrop
magnified to
dreadful clarity
    Sterile grain
    dumb apothecary
    fumes over the rim
    twist the air
        Sting the lip
        heat the temple
        the waiting door
        the clean razor

For an Addict

You'll choose a spot in a natural depression on a hill
You'll build a long, low house out of acacia wood
unconnected to the power grid

You'll live there with two other women, twenty white goats,
and seven dogs—Rottweiler, Schnauzer, Pug, Dalmatian,
Highland Terrier, Blue Healer, Kelpie

You'll fabricate tanks out of concrete to deal with waste
and a small igloo shaped building of red bricks
but you'll forget the purpose of it

You'll talk to people in town who will like you and visit
and when they visit you will offer them home brew
some of them will not understand

You'll discern a drumming, sweaty peace out of children
wild on the lawn at twilight and scraps of writing
pinned to grass trees by the wind

Peel Caravan Park, July 19, 2010

The disorganised July air lurks in corners
whispering secrets to sleeping air conditioners
scraping frost on a dormant red car bonnet
filling pit marks in pointless concrete slabs

Inside the ship-crate annex
it's three degrees colder than the grave
old couples grow micro gardens
succulents, maidenhair, fat pots of carnation
With less pretence, the grim and the vacant
smoke languidly in what sun is available

A percussion of small stones under tyres
shakes the metal walls of each van
a passing noted, secretly, by all
No lamb's blood on the sliding door
to turn this pinch faced angel away

In the middle distance a bearded man
who used to shave
sits twitching
framed by aluminium
wondering when
this transience became permanent

The Opposite of Dreaming

Day never breaks in winter
it only drips in
over the parapet
of a gummy, static night

Sticky dregs at the bottom
of a Salvation
Army sherry glass
with a dull, cream price tag

In a goblin nest of objects
the surface of a
picture studded
with crystalline pink specs

The serotonin pump drops
pressure and the
indifferent breeze
feels as good as kindness

Gunmetal morning kills each star
the glinting cascade
off a welding torch
going out on eternal concrete

Punding

after 'The Sleep Deprivation Diaries' *by Scott-Patrick Mitchell*

In the years that come, you'll remember a junkpile,
dump-truck planted at the edge of a peacock rug.
Plasma mists playing between accidental *objet d'art.*

Any shit-boring Thursday when you see a pilgrim
chewing the air, his afternoon schedule established
and filed in the zip-lock under shadow-people outgoings.

These are the times you'll look to where it lives
among a magpie trove of movie songs, gather to you
all the x and y to twist into a necklace for distant Morpheus.

In memory, deep as creases in that overworn shirt,
hand searching for sharp edges with a rictus smile,
where you and the imps flirted at the edge of a supernova.

At the Kakadu Mercure

Inside the crocodile, we look into the bartender's ear
for hidden galaxies as he bends over for lime slices.
Speckling dark wax continents reveal only a planet.
Floating on skin boats, signing Jonah's tight contract,
scoping for the *Deus* behind portals marked NO ENTRY
and finding another disappointing space-distortion inside—
trafficked cliff-faces of red and blue cleaning fluids.

Casino memories of our prosecco chatter company,
maintaining the holy losing streak, throwing money
down the soul-hole. Employ the sparkling fit-pack
in the pine-fresh toilets or the crystal pipe under
gorgeous light pollution in the carpark at three A.M.
We ended our pilgrimage where all faithful addicts go,
trapped in an effigy, quests abandoned by the ochre verge.

Under gas-fluorescence, Ken Done quilt covers quiver
and offer to roll us to oblivion in kitsch paint slashes.
Noblest of mini-bars, whisper of your legal comforts.
Baby-steps with tiny bottles, deliver us to bigger things.
King-Size-Twin pathos seeping through architecture,
we snaked aside the bone-nylon verticals with high-hope
and found serviceable French doors opening onto eternity.

Brick and Tile, 4 x 2, Cannington

I worked so hard that day,
it was a marvel to all
who saw me dashing
over the dusty building site.
        Grabbing the step ladder
        palm up—swinging
        at the balance point
        and moving off with it
        diagonal over my shoulder,
like a wuxia actor
taking up a weapon.
        I told them I was high on life
        and it was true—tinsel-giddy on
        a ten o'clock sunbreak in autumn.
But, also, off the crank I smoked
                from the mottled inside
                of a broken lightbulb,
                sweating in the PVC
                portable toilet unit.
                        Staring myself down
                        through the mirror's
                        blistered quicksilver.

A Song for Saint Roch

ekphrasis after 'Apples' *by Helen Grey-Smith, and* 'Saint Roch' *by Francisco Ribaltá*

I found two pristine cigarettes
in an old backpack I was clearing out.

In Helen's painting, two apples
nest in darker / lighter contrast.

Only a petite slash of the palette knife
and there's a stalk, offset into azure.

Could be a sky, but I see bourgeois
paint choices on new plaster.

Maybe some 4 x 2 x 2 cars x 2 kids
somewhere in garden stretches of outer Success

I found two pristine cigarettes
in an old backpack I was clearing out

Am I even seeing apples? Why should shape
dictate anything so fresh and healthy?

Maybe those Italian marzipan fruit
made for baroque festivals and saints

I never heard of, or that saint with
the boil on his inner thigh, dog waiting

to lick the thick pus that will
run down his holy, hairless leg.

I found two pristine cigarettes
in an old backpack I was clearing out

and I crushed up the packet in my fist.
They were too beautiful to look at.

PART SIX: MIDRASHIM

THE ANGEL

In baroque sheds, hard by economic ground zero, we theorized the angel.
Whistling policy bombs over scratchy grassed suburbs, sprinklers off
for the stretch of tyrant summer—too starved to offer the body moisture.
Riding surfboard thick soles down a wave of sticky tarmac; odyssey to
see the corpse of a god, its stretched form is a concrete tilt-slab shopping
gallery where we can buy—Gatorade (for restoration); sunglasses (for
hiding); solid food (for a time much later); mirrors (for fighting shadows).
Money gone before it's spent, air in our pockets vibrates with voices
yelping crude advice on socializing with store clerks, who might forgive
five cents from the price of a sports drink for all salt lost on the way.
These speakers are dead friends, ghosted down to shards and stimulated
dopamine receptors, shaken harder than forgetting's graced fingers
can grip; will to the void answered in heavy-metal volumes of memory.
Sing to me, O fuses, of all that's about to blow, of how we held our
seams in stitch among the pale Sunday travellers of suburban commerce
who sold and sold and bought on stolen plots near enough choking
road-ways that rode them to work, to feed back-monkeys pleasant goods
and such shiny stuff as the dreams-you-have-after-TV are made of.
Outside, clear proof—an insolent handprint pressed into young cement,
our blackening enamel smiles for just each other, traces of the angel.
We smoke among hairdressers, bakers, and squinting optometrists, out
far from the glass portals, under a multi-level car park where plastic
waste pipes grid and cross—mapping out past the place where stone cuts
into sun—paper, grease, shit, and soap flowing off to meet the light.

Platform Games

You feel the ancient cobblestones under your work-boots, steel-toe for kicking evil away. In the dripping, humid passage, you see a flicker of red and white. A mushroom speaks, *Thank you, Mario, but our princess is in another castle.*

A week ago, you were a plumber. Your hero's journey was only the smile a frustrated burgher offered when the pipes ran clear. Home on time to eat a warm dinner in front of the news. Weekend with the phone off for clean hands on a Sunday. It was sly chance that made you something different. Fifty paces on, the air is dense and each breath thick as custard. Sweat collects over your moustache and you almost trip on another mushroom. This one has a voice too, *Thank you, Mario, but the princess has rescued herself; all princesses are now self-rescuing.*

The chord of a story snaps around you. This or that, blue collar labourer or knight of the realm. Level up or drop the last life you have. When you sense a thinner atmosphere, when you can breathe the way you like, you make a choice for yourself. You pull the useless coins from your pocket and drop them in a rain of chimes and brass-sparks. One hits a third mushroom, who says, *Thank you, Mario, but the old world is dying and the new world is struggling to be born, now is the time of monsters.*

You ignore all three mushrooms, there is a light ahead.

An Uprising in York

Disappointed streetlights, leaking muntz-brass sick buzz-glow,
fail to push off a million-tonne night past the breathing tree line,
but speckle an intimate polish on the leader's boot, well dressed for revolution.

Christian soldiers of diverse heights swank up Avon Terrace wearing—
a buttoned business shirt; a grey singlet for penitence; budget sneakers.
Resolved to war, this past night of vigil—sleepless agape at the teacher's words.

Ordinance: eight dollars and fifty cents in change; two jack knives
between six men; oranges for half time; varicoloured water bottles;
tools for entry; an itemized manifesto; floppy vinyl covered King James Bible.

They take a back lane and declaim by the tradesmen's entrance
an indivisible republic of West'ralia, under the radiant sovereign,
then take rechargeable drills and proud crowbars to the ancient courthouse door.

Entering at sunrise, the leader takes the empty magistrate's throne,
and his deflating lungs echo in the disused heritage tourist attraction.
Camera-phone scans the vacant room, where they will rule colonial ghosts forever.

Power slumps from lamps outside, the bitumen reaches for the infinite.
Police sirens wake bats, only recently gone down and still remembering
last night's invisible song and flight; like fuzzy little gods over heaving wild-oats.

THE MAGIC FLUX

I knew a welder called Henry
who possessed a magical flux,
of his own manufacture,
that could facilitate the welding
of any metal to any other metal.

Whenever a stranger would ask
how the substance was made,
Henry would gather his co-workers,
stand on a chair (rightly above them),
and recite the following recipe.

Grind a powder from

Two skull fragments from a Neanderthal of either sex
Half a kilogram of blue asbestos
The fingernails of an executed thief
Eight petals from flowers found in Aztec Tombs
Rust from Excalibur

Two skull fragments from a Neanderthal of either sex
Half a kilogram of blue asbestos
The fingernails of an executed thief
Eight petals from flowers found in Aztec Tombs
Rust from Excalibur

Mix with

Two grams of pure Columbian cocaine
The dust from the surface of a mirror
Sand from the beaches of Normandy
Three tablespoons of baking powder
A handful of paint chips from any work of renaissance art

To form a paste add

The tears of your first-born child
Old, white paint found in a tin at the back of a shed
Sea water kept in a jam-jar for seven years
Two drops of Jesus Christ's semen

Agitate

There in the dim workshop
Something explodes like a firework over water:
the point Darwin missed.
Yes, we are monkeys,
but what fabulous monkeys we are.

AN EXTRACT

"The customer is the direction of your life. To be a customer is to receive, and to serve a customer is to give. Yet the customer, whether you or another being, gives currency in order to receive, and you, as seller, receive their currency in order to grant a customer's desire. The customer is a complete circle of the personal and the social, the self and the other, the want and the need.

Thus, the customer is not only defined by the moment of transaction. At the moment you are a customer you attain this place in transaction, and, at the moment the other buys from you, the other takes on the mantle that was once your own. At all times all humans are customers, their latent potential to buy is always present. In the way a divine nature is always ready to emerge in moral goodness and conformity when the chance to act well is presented, the customer nature is always ready to emerge when the chance to buy is present. You must love the customer as yourself, because you recognize the fragment of your commercial self in the customer. That is why we say, at Fragrant Home Centre, that seeing the face of a customer is like seeing the face of G-d."

—*From the introduction to* Fragrant Home Centre Orientation, *File 1, version 762.*

Studio Story

I was making a movie and a piss-bucket hung from the ceiling. The bucket was red and suspended from a rope of red hair. A thin mist of evaporating urine spiralled over the rim. The villain had set it as a trap for me, specifically. This is a writer / director / actor kind of thing. We on the same page? Glad we sorted that out.

The protagonist is dealing with suicidal ideation. I mean, that's entertaining, right? To be or to snatch it before closing time? Policeman with severe PTSD slips a 9mm-Ruger into his mouth, bringing his famous lips down on the gleaming, rectangular barrel. He hates himself and most of the world. The kids love that stuff.

This movie is all set-ups and McGuffins. It doesn't bend to that exposition-resolving-in-plot Malarkey. Instead, we plumb the mysteries of the in-between. You'd be right to think there's long scenes of the sun's edge travelling up a billowing gauze drape. It's unashamedly an art piece and a taste acquired by circuitous routes.

Last day of filming was the first, the crew worked chronologically backwards. Asking for pay before turning up, the denouement was shot before the script was written. A long clawed super-villain tipped the bucket on the hero. Rank ammonia soaked his virtue. Did I say hero? It's already the future, none of those left.

The camera panned to the past. Extended, sweeping panorama-frame. Over the heads of refugees staggering out of pogroms. Through the grind of a medieval battle with grey flashes from an overcast sky. Though space with that effect that elongates the stars. Somewhere still and ancient, an emotive orchestral track swells and rises.

A Prayer for Uniforms

You are a camera falling from a ceiling onto a data entry clerk. A faulty plaster screw pings under the tension of your left-right flex and you scan the whole expansive room for the first time since the day you were installed.

Forty-seven humans are peering at screens and pecking at keyboards, corralled behind cream rectangles, formal illusions of privacy under security optics. Sections of their beautiful costumes flash on your lens as you tumble.

Serious blacks and innocent browns; toothy whites and so much beige. Flesh coloured silk peeks over a waistband. You are spinning fast, end over end, so that you can't tell a pencil skirt from a pocket ripped off in mourning.

As you close with the clerk, whose ribs you will crush in less than a second, the weave of his shirt becomes visible. A broken thread begs to be pulled, unravelling the whole garment into a twine-cloud of soft entropy on the floor.

Just before impact, the threads are big as ropes—all knotted tendon. And whispering from the pages of unpublished novels hidden in their coils. The callous on a sailor's hand, the burn on a captive's wrist, the braid of a lover's hair.

TRANSLATING PSALMS FROM HEBREW

I am a man sitting on a
couch made in the nineteen-twenties, in a room
full of moths. I must write about the moths.

To describe the moths I cannot
look directly at them. I have to focus
on my notebook, so I only see lines.

But, occasionally, one drops
across my eye line, its long battle with the
electric light lost. I always catch it.

And hold it until its dun and
grey shades disintegrate or intensify;
until it becomes a chrysanthemum.

Fruit for Rosa

after 'This is Just to Say' *by William Carlos Williams*

I recommend, if you're going to eat plums,
to pick a plum that tastes so much like a plum
its juices coating your tongue
are like the fantastic dreams
of a corporate food-scientist
chasing artificial plum flavour,
        ending in a glorious rise to upper management.

That's your plum, pursue it everywhere,
even if its season lasts only an hour of summer.
See, in the single kilogram
you will eat the whole day,
the miracle of the leaning tree,
sugars rising for a touch of sun,
        the music of everything being exactly itself.

PART SEVEN: AGAINST POETRY

Praxis

When you
see something beautiful
always try to smash it to pieces
gather the diverse fragments in a bucket
and knead them into a mound of your own shit
smear it on the wall and wait for the light to hit it just so

Pinjarra Part 2

Eucalypt scent and ozone
off the running water in the Murray
across the street from another supermarket,
arranged in the formal stanzas
of most other supermarkets.
            Bag full of baking goods,
            cream-cheese for rugelach
            that come from dead-Europe
            which mum took us out from,
            not trusting the bastards
            who stained every street
            with our blood.
Every street here
is just as stained.

                Adorno said no poetry
                after Auschwitz, Celan
                showed there must be.

Every corner here,
just as stained, just
not our blood this time.

You know it's stolen, right? Taken at gunpoint, the whole thing.

Baudelaire and Freud liked to get into the Silver Sands Tavern around six, before all the tickets for Crazy Tuesday Chase the Ace were gone and they missed out on winning the meat-pack. But the draw wasn't until eight and five beers saw them propping up the bar in a bloated malaise, so that they couldn't stand to look at each other anymore, as much as they couldn't bear to talk another word. They turned, instead, to the inbuilt TAB. A giant, purple man in golden armour was betting on the greyhounds. With each dismal loss of a ten-dollar slip, he would mutter 'You dare defy a Titan?'

'I know this man,' Freud exclaimed. 'He is notorious.'

'Notorious he is,' Baudelaire gravely agreed. 'His mother spits on the ground where he was born and his children crawl the earth in numb despite. He is a searcher and it is the searcher who never arrives at his destination. Always another gamble, always another Four X, always another mystic gem. I know him, for I am the very scion of his colossal loin and he has cursed me with poetry.'

The purple man went out to smoke by the broad windows over Henson Street. He tapped his pack of Long Beach Gold with a finger like a tree limb, blowing math-shaped symbols off towards the yelling, chemical dawn that was slipping along under the qualified promises of night. Freud added a spec more cocaine to his Swan Draught, shrugged, and said 'Fuck, Charlie, do you actually mind? It's been a long day.'

A Final Word on William McGonagall

One thing McGonagall did was mention prices. You're not supposed to mention prices in a poem. I don't know who wrote the rule. But it somehow *sounds* wrong. The same rule applies in polite company. I found this out when I was overly proud of a linen shirt I got cheap. A rich woman sledgehammered me for saying what it cost in front of everyone. It was hard for me to know what I'd done wrong. I could never figure out what McGonagall was doing wrong either. I read him through a dozen times and each line is perfect.

Old Mate

Hello, you must have come while I was reading.
Midnight and silky,
I wanted to touch your fur—

or let you lick my face,
but I forgot your breath stunk like mass graves.
(Smell is three quarters of memory)

It's not my memory, why'd you bring it?
Normal visitors bring chocolate.
You brought cattle trains.

Yellow stars aren't candy.
You know where the levers are.
Look at you pulling them,
rank fucker.

But I'm not going to choke on you,
I'll give you a kiss—
for the songs you taught,
for the notes I can reach.

G-d, Sleep, and Chaos
by Alan Fyfe

Eulogy for Hasan (published in *Overland 239* and shortlisted for the Judith Wright Poetry Prize); A Hill Outside Yanchep (published in *Westerly 65.1* and republished in *Poetry for the Planet Anthology*); The Bin Truck Said (published in *Australian Poetry Journal Vol. 9*); Two Visitation Dreams (awarded second in the Tom Collins Poetry Prize); Ocean (published in *Overland 239*); St John's Wort (published in *Admissions: Voices Within Mental Health Anthology, Upswell 2022*); After Pittsburgh (published in *Australian Poetry Journal Vol. 12.1*); Ether (published in *Unlikely Stories IV*); Smash (published in *Poetry d'Amour Anthology*); Peel Caravan Park, July 29. 2010 (published in *Verseville Issue XXIX*); A Song for St Roch (published in *Westerly 67.2*); Platform Games (published in *Overland 248*); The Angel (shortlisted and commended in The Tom Collins Poetry Prize); A Prayer for Uniforms (published in *The LWAG Ekphrasis Project*); The Magic Flux (published in *Cottonmouth Journal*); Translating Psalms from Hebrew (published as 'The Translator' in *Cottonmouth Journal*); Towards Silence (published in *Unlikely Stories V*); *G-d, Sleep, and Chaos* (awarded the silver medal in the Flying Islands Unpublished Manuscript Award, also awarded in the WA Poets' Inc Emerging Poets Program)

First published 2024

POETRY

ISBN: 978-0-6459209-7-0

BOOK, TYPSETTING, AND LOGO DESIGN
Mountains Brown Press

PUBLISHER
Life Before Man

Gazebo Books
PO Box 375
Summer Hill
New South Wales 2130
Australia

gazebobooks.com.au

2 4 6 8 10 9 7 5 3 1

This book was made possible thanks to Anthony Mark Day

COVER IMAGE: *Her No. 2*, 2023, oil on canvas, 50 x 40 cm, © Phil Day

ISBN 978-0-6459209-7-0